Griffeth

Leaves of
Inspiration

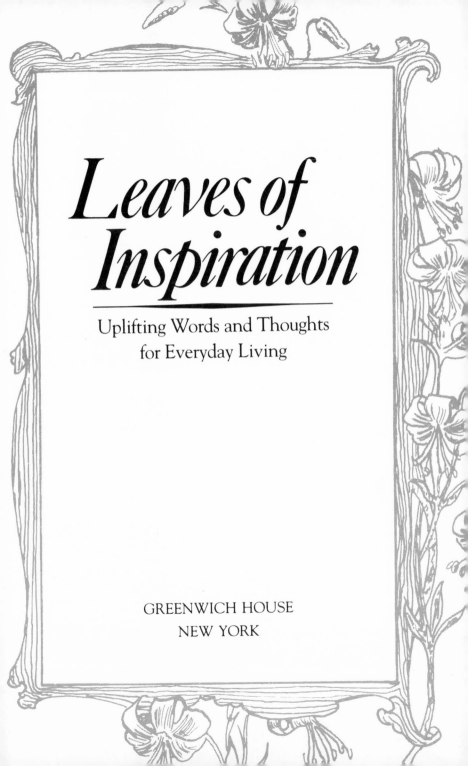

Leaves of Inspiration

Uplifting Words and Thoughts
for Everyday Living

GREENWICH HOUSE
NEW YORK

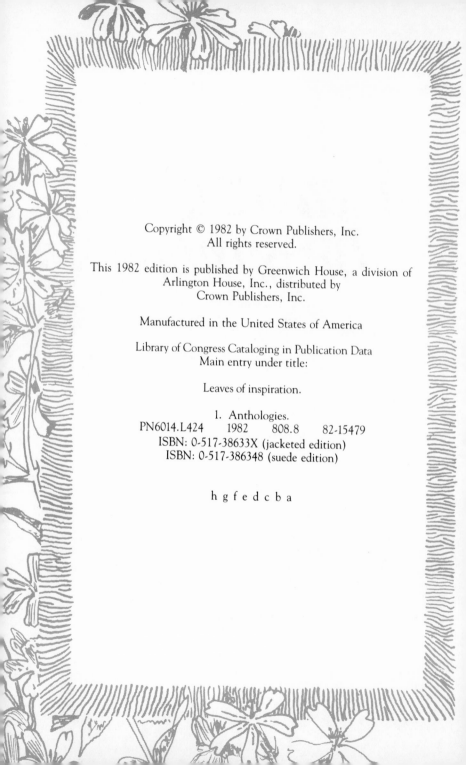

This 1982 edition is published by Greenwich House, a division of
Arlington House, Inc., distributed by
Crown Publishers, Inc.

Manufactured in the United States of America

Library of Congress Cataloging in Publication Data
Main entry under title:

Leaves of inspiration.

1. Anthologies.
PN6014.L424   1982   808.8   82-15479
ISBN: 0-517-38633X (jacketed edition)
ISBN: 0-517-386348 (suede edition)

h g f e d c b a

FOREWORD

"If you have built castles in the air,
Your work need not be lost;
That is where they should be.
Now put foundations under them."

Henry David Thoreau

The quotations gathered in *Leaves of Inspiration* are a unique collection, featuring the wisdom of great writers—Robert Louis Stevenson, Abraham Lincoln, Henry David Thoreau, Henry Van Dyke, Leonardo da Vinci, William Shakespeare, Sir Walter Scott and others. But the anonymous writer, the "little person," is also represented in this collection, each one revealing his original and sensitive insights into life.

The humdrum details of daily living can dull our senses and blind us to the full beauty and potential of life. Between earning a living, paying bills, running errands and just keeping body and soul together, we often feel as if we have no time or energy to realize our full potential as human beings or to develop our personal talents and gifts.

The quotations gathered here give us that extra push to achieve our goals; they remind us that an act of love, however small, enriches our life immeasurably. The authors quoted here were also people with too much to do, who at times undoubtedly felt overburdened and depressed by life.

But their gift was their ability to stop and recognize their true priorities, to show us that working toward a dream and caring for the people around us makes life a wonderful experience, not a drudgery to be endured.

These quotations motivate and encourage us; they lift our spirits after a hard day or an upsetting experience. By drawing us out of our self-absorption, *Leaves of Inspiration* shows us how delightful life is, how much happiness we can achieve if we not only build castles in the air but work at putting foundations under them.

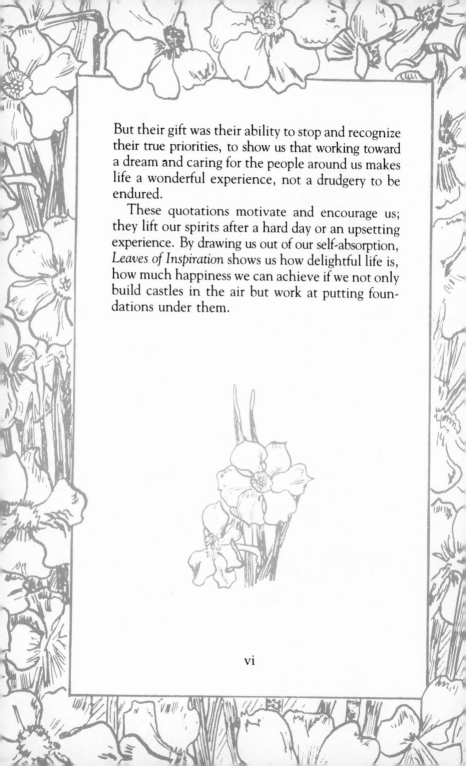

IF YOU HAVE BUILT CASTLES IN THE AIR

If you have built castles in the air,
　　Your work need not be lost;
　　that is where they should be.
Now put foundations under them.

Henry David Thoreau

FOR THOSE WHO FAIL

"All honor to him who shall win the prize,"
　　The world has cried for a thousand years,
But to him who tries and who fails and dies,
　　I give great honor and glory and tears.

Give glory and honor and pitiful tears
　　To all who fail in their deeds sublime,
Their ghosts are many in the van of years,
　　They were born with Time in advance of Time.

Oh, great is the hero who wins a name,
　　But greater many and many a time
Some pale-faced fellow who dies in shame
　　And lets God finish the thought sublime.

And great is the man with a sword undrawn,
　　And good is the man who refrains from wine;
But the man who fails and who still fights on,
　　Lo, he is the twin-brother of mine.

1

LET SOMETHING GOOD BE SAID

When over the fair fame of friend or foe
 The shadow of disgrace shall fall; instead
Of words of blame, or proof of so and so,
 Let something good be said.

Forget not that no fellow-being yet
 May fall so low but love may lift his head;
Even the cheek of shame with tears is wet,
 If something good be said.

No generous heart may vainly turn aside
 In ways of sympathy; no soul so dead
But may awaken strong and glorified,
 If something good be said.

And so I charge ye, by the thorny crown,
 And by the cross on which the Saviour bled,
And by your own soul's hope for fair renown,
 Let something good be said.

James Whitcomb Riley

LOOK UP!

 Look up! and not down;
 Out! and not in;
 Forward! and not back;
 And lend a hand.

2

THE FOOTPATH TO PEACE

To be glad of life, because it gives you the chance to love and to work and to play and to look up at the stars; to be satisfied with your possessions, but not contented with yourself until you have made the best of them; to despise nothing in the world except falsehood and meanness, and to fear nothing except cowardice; to be governed by your admirations rather than by your disgusts; to covet nothing that is your neighbor's except his kindness of heart and gentleness of manners; to think seldom of your enemies, often of your friends and every day of Christ; and to spend as much time as you can with body and with spirit, in God's out-of-doors—these are little guide-posts on the footpath to peace.

Henry Van Dyke

THANK GOD EVERY MORNING

Thank God every morning when you get up that you have something to do that day which must be done, whether you like it or not. Being forced to work, and forced to do your best, will breed in you temperance and self-control, diligence and strength of will, cheerfulness and content, and a hundred virtues which the idle never know.

3

THE WONDROUS CROSS

When I survey the wondrous cross
  On which the Prince of Glory died,
My richest gain I count but loss,
  And pour contempt on all my pride.

Forbid it, Lord! that I should boast,
  Save in the death of Christ, my God;
All the vain things that charm me most
  I sacrifice them to His blood.

See, from His head, His hands, His feet,
  Sorrow and love flow mingled down;
Did e'er such love and sorrows meet,
  Or thorns compose so rich a crown?

His dying crimson, like a robe,
  Spreads o'er His body on the tree;
Then I am dead to all the globe,
  And all the globe is dead to me.

Were the whole realm of nature mine,
  That were a present far too small;
Love so amazing, so divine,
  Demands my soul, my life, my all.

Isaac Watts

4

GIVE THEM THE FLOWERS NOW

Closed eyes can't see the white roses,
  Cold hands can't hold them, you know,
Breath that is stilled cannot gather
  The odors that sweet from them blow.
Death, with a peace beyond dreaming,
  Its children of earth doth endow;
Life is the time we can help them,
  So give them the flowers now!

Here are the struggles and striving,
  Here are the cares and the tears;
Now is the time to be smoothing
  The frowns and the furrows and fears.
What to closed eyes are kind sayings?
  What to hushed heart is deep vow?
Naught can avail after parting,
  So give them the flowers now!

GREAT MINDS

Great minds have purposes; little minds have
wishes. Little minds are subdued by misfortunes;
great minds rise above them.

Washington Irving

5

JOHN WESLEY'S RULE

Do all the good you can,
By all the means you can,
In all the ways you can,
In all the places you can,
At all the times you can,
To all the people you can,
As long as ever you can.

John Wesley

TRUE REST

Rest is not quitting
   The busy career;
Rest is the fitting
   Of self to one's sphere.

'Tis the brook's motion.
   Clear without strife,
Fleeting to ocean,
   After this life.

'Tis loving and serving,
   The highest and best;
'Tis onward, unswerving,
   And this is true rest.

Goethe

6

SUCCESS

Trifles make perfection, but perfection is no trifle.

Michelangelo

The word "success" appears but once in the Bible, in the following verse:

This book of the law shall not depart out of thy mouth; but thou shalt meditate therein day and night, that thou mayest observe to do according to all that is written therein: for then thou shalt make thy way prosperous, and then thou shalt have good success.

Joshua 1: 8

A ROSE TO THE LIVING

A rose to the living is more
    Than sumptuous wreaths to the dead;
In filling love's infinite store,
A rose to the living is more
If graciously given before
    The hungering spirit is fled—
A rose to the living is more
    Than sumptuous wreaths to the dead.

ONE HOUR OF LIFE

One hour of life, crowded to the full with glorious action, and filled with noble risks, is worth whole years of those mean observances of petty decorum, in which men steal through existence, like sluggish waters through a marsh, without either honor or observation.

Sir Walter Scott

FAME

The heights by great men reached and kept
   Were not attained by sudden flight,
But they while their companions slept
   Were toiling upward in the night.

Henry W. Longfellow

SPANISH PROVERB

The pleasures of the senses pass quickly; those of the heart become sorrows, but those of the mind are ever with us, even to the end of our journey.

LITTLE BY LITTLE

Little by little the time goes by—
Short, if you sing through it, long, if you sigh,
Little by little—an hour a day,
Gone with the years that have vanished away.
Little by little the race is run;
Trouble and waiting and toil are done!

Little by little the skies grow clear;
Little by little the sun comes near;
Little by little the days smile out,
Gladder and brighter on pain and doubt;
Little by little the seed we sow
Into a beautiful yield will grow.

Little by little the world grows strong,
Fighting the battle of Right and Wrong;
Little by little the Wrong gives way—
Little by little the Right has sway.
Little by little all longing souls
Struggle up nearer the shining goals.

Little by little the good in men
Blossoms to beauty, for human ken;
Little by little the angels see
Prophecies better of good to be;
Little by little the God of all
Lifts the world nearer the pleading call.

IS IT WORTH WHILE?

Is it worth while that we jostle a brother,
  Bearing his load on the rough road of life?
Is it worth while that we jeer at each other—
  In blackness of heart, that we war to the knife?
  God pity us all in our pitiful strife.

God pity us all as we jostle each other;
  God pardon us all for the triumph we feel
When a fellow goes down 'neath his load on the
    heather,
  Pierced to the heart: Words are keener than steel,
  And mightier far for woe than for weal.

Were it not well, in this brief little journey
  On over the isthmus, down into the tide,
We give him a fish instead of a serpent,
  Ere folding the hands to be and abide
  Forever and aye in dust at his side?

Look at the roses saluting each other;
  Look at the herds all at peace on the plain;
Man, and man only, makes war on his brother,
  And laughs in his heart at his peril and pain—
  Shamed by the beasts that go down on the plain.

Is it worth while that we battle to humble
  Some poor fellow down into the dust?
God pity us all! Time too soon will tumble
  All of us together, like leaves in a gust,
  Humbled, indeed, down into the dust.

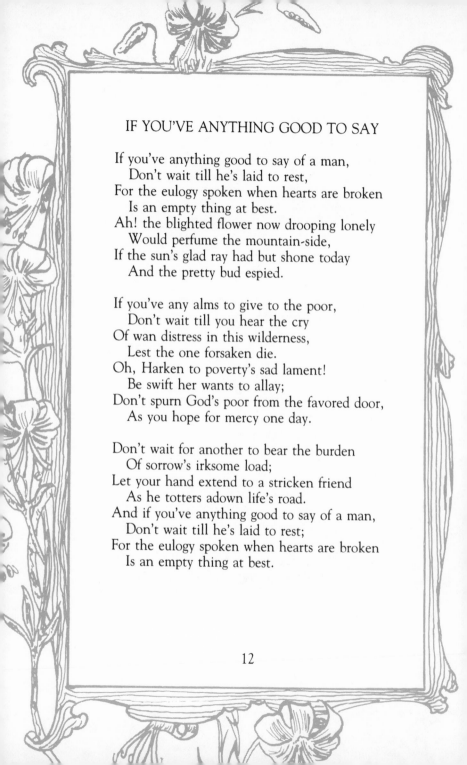

IF YOU'VE ANYTHING GOOD TO SAY

If you've anything good to say of a man,
   Don't wait till he's laid to rest,
For the eulogy spoken when hearts are broken
   Is an empty thing at best.
Ah! the blighted flower now drooping lonely
   Would perfume the mountain-side,
If the sun's glad ray had but shone today
   And the pretty bud espied.

If you've any alms to give to the poor,
   Don't wait till you hear the cry
Of wan distress in this wilderness,
   Lest the one forsaken die.
Oh, Harken to poverty's sad lament!
   Be swift her wants to allay;
Don't spurn God's poor from the favored door,
   As you hope for mercy one day.

Don't wait for another to bear the burden
   Of sorrow's irksome load;
Let your hand extend to a stricken friend
   As he totters adown life's road.
And if you've anything good to say of a man,
   Don't wait till he's laid to rest;
For the eulogy spoken when hearts are broken
   Is an empty thing at best.

LET US SMILE

The thing that goes the farthest towards making
   life worth while,
That costs the least and does the most, is just a
   pleasant smile,
The smile that bubbles from a heart that loves its
   fellowmen
Will drive away the cloud of gloom and coax the
   sun again,
It's full of worth and goodness, too, with manly
   kindness blent—
It's worth a million dollars, and doesn't cost a cent.

CHARITY

There is so much that is bad in the best of us
And so much that is good in the worst of us
That it doesn't behoove any of us
To talk about the rest of us.

DO IT NOW

I expect to pass through this world but once.
Any good thing, therefore, that I can do or any
kindness I can show to any fellow human being
let me do it now. Let me not defer nor neglect it,
for I shall not pass this way again.

SHAKESPEARE'S WISDOM

And these few precepts in thy memory
See thou character. Give thy thoughts no tongue,
Nor any unproportioned thought his act.
Be thou familiar, but by no means vulgar.
Those friends thou hast, and their adoption tried,
Grapple them to thy soul with hoops of steel,
But do not dull thy palm with entertainment
Of each new-hatched unfledged comrade. Beware
of entrance to a quarrel; but being in,
Bear't, that the opposed may beware of thee.
Give every man thy ear, but few thy voice:
Take each man's censure, but reserve thy judgment.
Costly thy habit as thy purse can buy,
But not expressed in fancy; rich, not gaudy:
For the apparel oft proclaims the man;
And they in France of the best rank and station
Are of a most select and generous chief in that.
Neither a borrower nor a lender be:
For loan oft loses both itself and friend,
And borrowing dulls the edge of husbandry.
This above all: to thine own self be true,
And it must follow, as the night the day,
Thou canst not then be false to any man.

William Shakespeare

SPEAK GENTLY

Speak gently; it is better far
   To rule by love than fear;
Speak gently; let no harsh word mar
   The good we may do here.
Speak gently to the little child;
   Its love is sure to gain;
Teach it in accents soft and mild;
   It may not long remain.

Speak gently to the young, for they
   Will have enough to bear;
Pass through this life as best they may,
   'Tis full of anxious care,
Speak gently to the aged one,
   Grieve not the careworn heart,
Whose sands of life are nearly run:
   Let such in peace depart.

Speak gently to the erring; know
   They must have toiled in vain;
Perchance unkindness made them so;
   Oh, win them back again!
Speak gently; 'tis a little thing
   Dropped in the heart's deep well;
The good, the joy, that it may bring,
   Eternity shall tell.

FOR ALL THESE

I thank Thee, Lord, that I am straight and strong,
  With wit to work and hope to keep me brave;
That two score years, unfathomed, still belong
  To the allotted life Thy bounty gave.

I thank Thee that the sight of sunlit lands
  And dipping hills, the breath of evening grass—
That wet, dark rocks and flowers in my hands
  Can give me daily gladness as I pass.

I thank Thee that I love the things of Earth—
  Ripe fruits and laughter, lying down to sleep,
The shine of lighted towns, the graver worth
  Of beating human hearts that laugh and weep.

I thank Thee that as yet I need not know,
  Yet need not fear the mystery of end:
But more than all, and though all these should go—
  Dear Lord, this on my knees!—I thank Thee for
my friend.

FRIENDSHIP

So long as we love, we serve. So long as we are
loved by others I would almost say we were indis-
pensable; and no man is useless while he has a
friend.

Robert Louis Stevenson

16

I WOULD, DEAR JESUS

I would, dear Jesus, I could break
The hedge that creeds and hearsay make,
And, like the first disciples, be
In person led and taught by thee.

I read thy words, so strong and sweet;
I seek the footprints of thy feet;
But men so mystify the trace,
I long to see thee face to face.

Wouldst thou not let me at thy side,
In thee, in thee so sure confide?
Like John, upon thy breast recline,
And feel thy heart make mine divine?

CHANNING'S SYMPHONY

To live content with small means; to seek elegance
rather than luxury; and refinement rather than
fashion; to be worthy, not respectable; and wealthy,
not rich; to study hard, think quietly, talk gently,
act frankly; to listen to stars and birds, to babes
and sages, with open heart; to bear all cheerfully,
do all bravely, await occasion, hurry never; in a
word, to let the spiritual, unbidden and unconscious
grow up through the common. This is to be my
symphony.

William Henry Channing

WORK THOU FOR PLEASURE

Work thou for pleasure; paint or sing or carve
The thing thou lovest, though the body starve.
Who works for glory misses oft the goal;
Who works for money coins his very soul.
Work for work's sake then, and it well may be
That these things shall be added unto thee.

THANKFULNESS

Many favours which God giveth us ravel out for
want of hemming, through our own unthankfulness;
for though prayer purchaseth blessings, giving praise
doth keep the quiet possession of them.

Thomas Fuller

PLUCK WINS

Pluck wins! It always wins! though days be slow
And nights be dark 'twixt days that come and go.
Still pluck will win; its average is sure;
He gains the prize who will the most endure;
Who faces issues; he who never shirks;
Who waits and watches, and who always works.

WHAT HAVE WE DONE TODAY?

We shall do so much in the years to come,
  But what have we done today?
We shall give our gold in a princely sum,
  But what did we give today?
We shall lift the heart and dry the tear,
We shall plant a hope in the place of fear,
We shall speak the words of love and cheer,
  But what did we speak today?

We shall be so kind in the afterwhile,
  But what have we been today?
We shall bring each lonely life a smile,
  But what have we brought today?
We shall give to truth a grander birth,
And to steadfast faith a deeper worth,
We shall feed the hungering souls of earth,
  But whom have we fed today?

We shall reap such joys in the by and by,
  But what have we sown today?
We shall build us mansions in the sky,
  But what have we built today?
'Tis sweet in idle dreams to bask,
But here and now do we do our task?
Yes, this is the thing our souls must ask,
  "What have we done today?"

THE WORLD IS WAITING FOR YOU

The world is waiting for you, young man,
   If your purpose is strong and true;
If out of your treasures of mind and heart,
   You can bring things old and new,
If you know the truth that makes men free,
   And with skill can bring it to view,
The world is waiting for you, young man,
   The world is waiting for you.

There are treasures of mountain and treasures of
      sea,
   And harvest of valley and plain,
That Industry, Knowledge and Skill can secure,
   While Ignorance wishes in vain.
To scatter the lightning and harness the storm,
   Is a power that is wielded by few;
If you have the nerve and the skill, young man,
   The world is waiting for you.

Of the idle and brainless the world has enough—
   Who eat what they never have earned;
Who hate the pure stream from the fountain of
      truth,
   And wisdom and knowledge have spurned.
But patience and purpose which know no defeat,
   And genius like gems bright and true,
Will bless all mankind with their love, life and
      light,—
   The world is waiting for you.

20

Then awake, O young man, from the stupor of
  doubt
  And prepare for the battle of life;
Be the fire of the forge, or be anvil or sledge,—
  But win, or go down in the strife!
Can you stand though the world into ruin should
  rock?
  Can you conquer with many or few?
Then the world is waiting for you, young man,
  The world is waiting for you!

THE SAYING OF OMAR IBN AL HALIF

The Second Caliph

Four things come not back:
The spoken word;
The sped arrow;
Time past;
The neglected opportunity.

TODAY!

With every rising of the sun
Think of your life as just begun.

The Past has cancelled and buried deep
All yesterdays. There let them sleep.

Concern yourself with but Today.
Grasp it, and teach it to obey

Your will and plan. Since time began
Today has been the friend of man.

You and Today! A soul sublime
And the great heritage of time.

With God himself to bind the twain,
Go forth, brave heart! Attain! attain!

BE STRONG!

Be strong!
We are not here to play—to dream, to drift.
We have hard work to do and loads to lift.
Shun not the struggle—face it; 'tis God's gift.

Be strong!
Say not the days are evil. Who's to blame?
And fold the hands and acquiesce—O shame!
Stand up, speak out, and bravely, in God's name.

Be strong!
It matters not how deep intrenched the wrong,
How hard the battle goes, the day how long;
Faint not—fight on! Tomorrow comes the song.

WHAT OTHERS MAY NOT SEE!

If each man's secret, unguessed care
    Were written on his brow,
How many would our pity share
    Who have our envy now!
And if the promptings of each heart
    No artifice concealed,
How many trusting friends would part
    At what they saw revealed!

CONSEQUENCES

A traveler on a dusty road
    Strewed acorns on the lea;
And one took root and sprouted up,
    And grew into a tree.
Love sought its shade at evening time,
    To breathe his early vows.
And age was pleased, in heats of noon
    To bask beneath its boughs;
The dormouse loved its dangling twigs,
    The birds sweet music bore;
It stood a glory in its place,
    A blessing evermore.

A little spring had lost its way
    Amid the grass and fern;
A passing stranger scooped a well
    Where weary men might turn.
He walled it in, and hung with care
    A ladle at the brink;
He thought not of the deed he did,
    But judged that all might drink.
He paused again, and lo! the well,
    By summer never dried,
Had cooled ten thousand parching tongues
    And saved a life beside.

A dreamer dropped a random thought;
    'Twas old, and yet 'twas new;
A simple fancy of the brain,
    But strong in being true.

It shone upon a genial mind,
   And lo! its light became
A lamp of life, a beacon ray,
   A monitory flame.
The thought was small, its issue great;
   A watch-fire on the hill;
It shed its radiance far adown,
   And cheers the valley still.

A nameless man, amid a crowd
   That thronged the daily mart,
Let fall a word of Hope and Love,
   Unstudied from the heart;
A whisper on the tumult thrown,
   A transitory breath—
It raised a brother from the dust,
   It saved a soul from death.
O germ! O fount! O word of love!
   O thought at random cast!
Ye were but little at the first,
   But mighty at the last.

HULLO!

When you see a man in woe,
Walk straight up and say, "Hullo!"
Say, "Hullo!" and "How d'ye do?
How's the world been using you?"
Slap the fellow on his back,
Bring your hand down with a whack;
Waltz straight up and don't go slow,
Shake his hand and say, "Hullo!"

Is he clothed in rags? Oh, ho!
Walk straight up and say, "Hullo!"
Rags are but a cotton roll
Just for wrapping up a soul;
And a soul is worth a true
Hale and hearty "How d'ye do?"
Don't wait for the crowd to go;
Walk straight up and say, "Hullo!"

When big vessels meet, they say,
They salute and sail away:
Just the same as you and me,
Lonely ships upon the sea,
Each one sailing his own jog
For a port beyond the fog;
Let your speaking-trumpet blow,
Lift your horn and cry, "Hullo!"

Say "Hullo!" and "How d'ye do?"
Other folks are good as you.
When you leave your house of clay,
Wandering in the far away;
When you travel through the strange
Country far beyond the range,
Then the souls you've cheered will know
Who you be, and say, "Hullo!"

GIVE THEM THE FLOWERS NOW

Closed eyes can't see the white roses,
  Cold hands can't hold them, you know,
Breath that is stilled cannot gather
  The odors that sweet from them blow.
Death, with a peace beyond dreaming,
  Its children of each doth endow;
Life is the time we can help them,
  So give them the flowers now!

Here are the struggles and striving,
  Here are the cares and the tears;
Now is the time to be smoothing
  The frowns and the furrows and fears.
What to closed eyes are kind sayings?
  What to hushed heart is deep vow?
Naught can avail after parting,
  So give them the flowers now!

Just a kind word or a greeting;
  Just a warm grasp or a smile—
These are the flowers that will lighten
  The burdens for many a mile.
After the journey is over
  What is the use of them; how
Can they carry them who must be carried?
  Oh, give them the flowers now!

Blooms from the happy heart's garden
   Plucked in the spirit of love;
Blooms that are earthly reflections
   Of flowers that blossom above.
Words cannot tell what a measure
   Of blessings such gifts will allow
To dwell in the lives of many,
   So give them the flowers now!

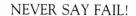

NEVER SAY FAIL!

Keep pushing—'tis wiser
   Than sitting aside,
And dreaming and sighing,
   And waiting the tide.
In life's earnest battle
   They only prevail
Who daily march onward
   And never say fail!

With an eye ever open,
   A tongue that's not dumb,
And a heart that will never
   To sorrow succumb—
You'll battle and conquer,
   Though thousands assail:
How strong and how mighty
   Who never say fail!

The spirit of angels
   Is active, I know,
As higher and higher
   In glory they go;
Methinks on bright pinions
   From Heaven they sail,
To cheer and encourage
   Who never say fail!

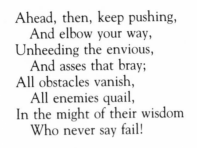

Ahead, then, keep pushing,
   And elbow your way,
Unheeding the envious,
   And asses that bray;
All obstacles vanish,
   All enemies quail,
In the might of their wisdom
   Who never say fail!

In life's early morning,
   In manhood's firm pride,
Let this be your motto
   Your footsteps to guide;
In storm and in sunshine,
   Whatever assail,
We'll onward and conquer,
   And never say fail!

LINCOLN'S RULES FOR LIVING

   Do not worry, eat three square meals a day, say
your prayers, be courteous to your creditors, keep
your digestion good, steer clear of biliousness, ex-
ercise, go slow and go easy. May be there are other
things that your special case requires to make you
happy, but, my friend, these I reckon will give you
a good lift.

Abraham Lincoln

I RESOLVE

To keep my health;
To do my work;
To live;
To see to it I grow and gain and give;
Never to look behind me for an hour;
To wait in meekness, and to walk in power;
But always fronting onward to the light,
Always and always facing toward the right.
Robbed, starved, defeated, fallen, wide-astray—
On, with what strength I have;
Back to the way.

IN A FRIENDLY SORT O' WAY

When a man ain't got a cent, and he's feeling kind
o' blue,
An' the clouds hang dark an' heavy, an' won't let
the sunshine through,
It's a great thing, O my brethren, for a feller just
to lay
His hand upon your shoulder in a friendly sort o'
way!
It makes a man feel curious, it makes the teardrop
start,
An' you sort o' feel a flutter in the region of the
heart:
You can look up and meet his eyes; you don't know
what to say
When his hand is on your shoulder in a friendly
sort o' way.

Oh, the world's a curious compound, with its honey
and its gall,
With its cares and bitter crosses, but a good world,
after all.
An' a good God must have made it—leastways,
that is what I say,
When a hand is on my shoulder in a friendly sort
o' way.

James Whitcomb Riley

NOBILITY

True worth is in being, not seeming;
  In doing each day that goes by,
Some little good—not in dreaming
  Of great things to do by and by.
For whatever men say in their blindness.
  And spite of the fancies of youth,
There's nothing so kingly as kindness,
  And nothing so royal as truth.

We get back our mete as we measure:
  We cannot do wrong and feel right;
Nor can we give pain and gain pleasure,
  For justice avenges each slight.
The air for the wing of the sparrow,
  The bush for the robin and wren,
But always the path that is narrow
  And straight for the children of men.

We cannot make bargains for blisses,
  Nor catch them like fishes in nets,
And sometimes the thing our life misses
  Helps more than the thing which it gets.
For good lieth not in pursuing,
  Nor gaining of great nor of small;
But just in the doing—and doing
  As we would be done by, is all.

Through envy, through malice, through hating
　　Against the world early and late,
No jot of our courage abating,
　　Our part is to work and to wait.
And slight is the sting of his trouble
　　Whose winnings are less than his worth;
For he who is honest is noble,
　　Whatever his fortunes or birth.

Alice Cary

JUNE

And what is so rare as a day in June?
   Then, if ever, come perfect days;
Then heaven tries the earth if it be in tune,
   And over it softly her warm ear lays;
Whether we look, or whether we listen,
We hear life murmur, or see it glisten;
Every clod feels a stir of might.
   An instinct within it that reaches and towers,
And, groping blindly above it for light,
   Climbs to a soul in grasses and flowers;
The flush of life may well be seen
   Thrilling back over hills and valleys;
The cowslip startles in meadows green,
   The buttercup catches the sun in its chalice,
And there's never a leaf nor a blade too mean
   To be some happy creature's palace;
The little bird sits at his door in the sun,
   Atilt like a blossom among the leaves,
And lets his illumined being o'errun
   With the deluge of summer it receives;
His mate feels the eggs beneath her wings,
And the heart in her dumb breast flutters and sings;
He sings to the wide world, and she to her nest—
In the nice ear of nature, which song is the best?

James Russell Lowell

36

SEND THEM TO BED WITH A KISS

O mothers, so weary, discouraged,
   Worn out with the cares of the day,
You often grow cross and impatient,
   Complain of the noise and the play;
For the day brings so many vexations,
   So many things going amiss;
But, mothers, whatever may vex you,
   Send the children to bed with a kiss!

The dear little feet wander often,
   Perhaps, from the pathway of right,
The dear little hands find new mischief
   To try you from morning till night;
But think of the desolate mothers
   Who'd give all the world for your bliss,
And, as thanks for your infinite blessings,
   Send the children to bed with a kiss!

For some day their noise will not vex you,
   The silence will hurt you far more;
You will long for their sweet childish voices,
   For a sweet childish face at the door;
And to press a child's face to your bosom,
   You'd give all the world for just this!
For the comfort 'twill bring you in sorrow,
   Send the children to bed with a kiss!

BEGIN AGAIN

Every day is a fresh beginning,
  Every morn is the world made new;
You who are weary of sorrow and sinning,
  Here is a beautiful hope for you—
  A hope for me and a hope for you.

All the past things are past and over,
  The tasks are done and the tears are shed;
Yesterday's errors let yesterday cover;
  Yesterday's wounds, which smarted and bled,
  Are healed with the healing which night has shed.

Yesterday now is a part of forever,
  Bound up in a sheaf, which God holds tight;
With glad days and sad days and bad days which
    never
  Shall visit us more with their bloom and their
    blight,
  Their fullness of sunshine or sorrowful night.

Let them go, since we cannot relive them,
  Cannot undo, and cannot atone;
God in His mercy, receive, forgive them;
  Only the new days are our own,
  Today is ours, and today alone.

Here are the skies all burnished brightly,
  Here is the spent Earth all reborn,
Here are the tired limbs springing lightly
  To face the sun and to share with the morn,
  In the chrism of dew and the cool of dawn.

Every day is a fresh beginning;
  Listen, my soul, to the glad refrain,
And, spite of old sorrow and older sinning,
  And puzzles forecasted and possible pain,
  Take heart with the day, and begin again.

IF WE KNEW

If we knew the cares and crosses
   Crowding round our neighbor's way;
If we knew the little losses,
   Sorely grievous day by day,
Would we then so often chide him
   For the lack of thrift and gain—
Casting o'er his life a shadow,
   Leaving on his heart a stain.

If we knew the silent story
   Quivering through the heart of pain,
Would our womanhood dare doom them
   Back to haunts of guilt again?
Life hath many a tangled crossing,
   Joy hath many a break of woe,
And the cheeks tear-washed seem whitest,
   This the blessed angels know.

Let us reach into our bosoms
   For the key to other lives,
And with love to erring nature,
   Cherish good that still survives;
So that when our disrobed spirits
   Soar to realms of light again,
We may say, dear Father, judge us
   As we judged our fellowmen.

PER PACEM AD LUCEM

I do not ask, O Lord, that life should always be
        A pleasant road;
I do not ask that Thou shouldst take from me
        Aught of its load.
I do not ask that flowers should always spring
        Beneath my feet—
Too well I know the poison and the sting
        Of things too sweet.

For one thing only, Lord, dear Lord, I plead—
        Lead me aright,
Though strength should falter and though heart
   should bleed—
        Through peace to light.

I do not ask my cross to understand,
        My way to see;
Better in darkness just to feel Thy hand
        And follow Thee.

I do not ask that Thou shouldst always shed
        Full radiance here;
Give but a ray of peace that I may walk
        Without a fear.

Joy is like restless day, but Peace divine
        Like quiet night.
Lead me, O Lord, till perfect day shall shine
        Through Peace to Light.

WHAT I LIVE FOR

I live for those who love me,
  Whose hearts are kind and true,
For the heaven that smiles above me,
  And awaits my spirit, too;
For the human ties that bind me,
For the task by God assigned me,
For the bright hopes left behind me,
  And the good that I can do.

I live to learn their story
  Who've suffered for my sake,
To emulate their glory,
  And to follow in their wake;
Bards, patriots, martyrs, sages,
The noble of all ages,
Whose deeds crowd history's pages
  And Time's great volume make.

I live to hold communion
  With all that is divine,
To feel there is a union
  'Twixt Nature's heart and mine;
To profit by affliction,
Reap truths from fields of fiction,
Grow wiser from conviction,
  And fulfill each grand design.

I live to hail that season,
 By gifted minds foretold,
When men shall rule by reason,
 And not alone by gold;
When man to man united,
And every wrong thing righted,
The whole world shall be lighted
 As Eden was of old.

I live for those who love me,
 For those who know me true,
For the Heaven that smiles above me,
 And awaits my spirit, too;
For the cause that lacks assistance,
For the wrong that needs resistance,
For the future in the distance,
 And the good that I can do.

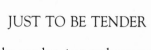

JUST TO BE TENDER

Just to be tender, just to be true,
Just to be glad the whole day through,
Just to be merciful, just to be mild,
Just to be trustful as a child;
Just to be gentle and kind and sweet,
Just to be helpful with willing feet,
Just to be cheery when things go wrong,
Just to drive sadness away with song,
Whether the hour is dark or bright,
Just to be loyal to God and right,
Just to believe that God knows best,
Just in his promises ever to rest
Just to let love be our daily key,
That is God's will for you and me.

A MORNING PRAYER

The day returns and brings us the petty round
of irritating concerns and duties. Help us to play
the man, help us to perform them with laughter
and kind faces, let cheerfulness abound with industry. Give us to go blithely on our business all
this day, bring us to our resting beds weary and
content and undishonored, and grant us in the end
the gift of sleep.

Robert Louis Stevenson

44

LEAD, KINDLY LIGHT

Lead, kindly Light, amid the encircling gloom,
    Lead thou me on!
The night is dark, and I am far from home—
    Lead thou me on!
Keep thou my feet; I do not ask to see
The distant scene—one step enough for me.

I was not ever thus, nor prayed that thou
    Shouldst lead me on.
I loved to choose and see my path; but now
    Lead thou me on!
I loved the garish day, and, spite of fears,
Pride ruled my will; remember not past years.

So long they power hath blest me, sure it still
    Will lead me on,
O'er moor and fen, o'er crag and torrent, till
    The night is gone;
And with the morn those angel faces smile
Which I have loved long since and lost awhile.

Cardinal (John Henry) Newman

O Lord, thou givest us everything,
at the price of an effort.

Leonardo da Vinci

IF ALL WHO HATE WOULD LOVE US

If all who hate would love us,
    And all our loves were true,
The stars that swing above us
    Would brighten in the blue;
If cruel words were kisses,
    And every scowl a smile,
A better world than this is,
    Would hardly be worth while.
If purses would not tighten
    To meet a brother's need,
The load we bear would lighten
    Above the grave of greed.

If those who whine would whistle,
    And those who languish laugh,
The rose would rout the thistle,
    The grain outrun the chaff;
If hearts were only jolly,
    If grieving were forgot,
And tears of melancholy
    Were things that now are not;
Then love would kneel to duty,
    And all the world would seem
A bridal bower of beauty,
    A dream within a dream.

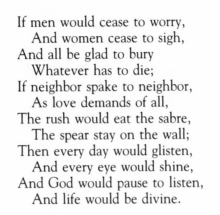

If men would cease to worry,
  And women cease to sigh,
And all be glad to bury
  Whatever has to die;
If neighbor spake to neighbor,
  As love demands of all,
The rush would eat the sabre,
  The spear stay on the wall;
Then every day would glisten,
  And every eye would shine,
And God would pause to listen,
  And life would be divine.

47

IF YOU HAVE A FRIEND WORTH LOVING

If you have a friend worth loving,
   Love him. Yes, and let him know
That you love him, ere life's evening
   Tinge his brow with sunset glow.
Why should good words ne'er be said
Of a friend—till he is dead?

If you hear a song that thrills you,
   Sung by any child of song,
Praise it. Do not let the singer
   Wait deservèd praises long.
Why should one who thrills your heart
Lack the joy you may impart?

If you hear a prayer that moves you
   By its humble, pleading tone,
Join it. Do not let the seeker
   Bow before his God alone.
Why should not your brother share
The strength of "two or three" in prayer?

If you see the hot tears falling
   From a brother's weeping eyes,
Share them. And by kindly sharing
   Own your kinship in the skies.
Why should anyone be glad
When a brother's heart is sad?

If a silvery laugh goes rippling
   Through the sunshine on his face,
Share it. 'Tis the wise man's saying—
   For both grief and joy a place.
There's health and goodness in the mirth
In which an honest laugh has birth.

If your work is made more easy
   By a friendly, helping hand,
Say so. Speak out brave and truly
   Ere the darkness veil the land.
Should a brother workman dear
Falter for a word of cheer?

Scatter thus your seeds of kindness
   All enriching as you go—
Leave them. Trust the Harvest-Giver;
   He will make each seed to grow.
So, until the happy end,
Your life shall never lack a friend.

SOMEBODY

Somebody did a golden deed;
Somebody proved a friend in need;
Somebody sang a beautiful song;
Somebody smiled the whole day long;
Somebody thought, " 'Tis sweet to live";
Somebody said, "I'm glad to give";
Somebody fought a valiant fight;
Somebody lived to shield the right;
    Was that "somebody" you?

A READER'S PRAYER

Lord, let me never slight the meaning nor the moral of anything I read. Make me respect my mind so much that I dare not read what has no meaning or moral. Help me choose with equal care my friends and my books, because they are both for life. Show me that as in a river, so in reading, the depths hold more of strength and beauty than the shallows. Teach me to value art without being blind to thought. Keep me from caring more for much reading than for careful reading; for books than the Book. Give me an ideal that will let me read only the best, and when that is done, stop me. Repay me with power to teach others, and then help me to say from a disciplined mind a grateful Amen.

OPPORTUNITY

Master of human destinies am I.
Fame, love, and fortune on my footsteps wait,
Cities and fields I walk; I penetrate
Deserts and seas remote, and, passing by
Hovel, and mart, and palace, soon or late
I knock unbidden once at every gate!
If sleeping, wake—if feasting, rise before

I turn away. It is the hour of fate,
And they who follow me reach every state
Mortals desire, and conquer every foe
Save death; but those who doubt or hesitate,
Condemned to failure, penury and woe,
Seek me in vain and uselessly implore,
I answer not, and I return no more.

TAKEN AT THE FLOOD

There is a tide in the affairs of men
Which, taken at the flood, leads on to fortune;
Omitted, all the voyage of their life
Is bound in shallows and in miseries.
On such a full sea are we now afloat,
And we must take the current when it serves,
Or lose our ventures.

Shakespeare

THE LORD'S PRAYER

After this manner therefore pray ye:
Our Father which art in heaven, hallowed be
Thy name. Thy kingdom come. Thy will be done
on earth as it is in heaven. Give us this day our
daily bread. And forgive us our debts, as we forgive
our debtors. And lead us not into temptation, but
deliver us from evil; for Thine is the kingdom, and
the power and the glory, forever. Amen.

Matthew 6: 9-13

GRATITUDE TO GOD

Notwithstanding all that I have suffered, notwithstanding all the pain and weariness and anxiety
and sorrow that necessarily enter into life, and the
inward errings that are worse than all, I would end
my record with a devout thanksgiving to the great
Author of my being. For more and more am I
unwilling to make my gratitude to Him what is
commonly called "a thanksgiving for mercies,"—
for any benefits or blessings that are peculiar to
myself, or my friends, or indeed to any man. Instead
of this, I would have it to be gratitude for all that
belongs to my life and being—for joy and sorrow,
for health and sickness, for success and disappoint-
ment, for virtue and for temptation, for life and
death; because I believe that all is meant for good.

THE INEVITABLE

I like the man who faces what he must
    With step triumphant and a heart of cheer;
    Who fights the daily battle without fear;
Sees his hopes fail, yet keeps unfaltering trust
That God is God; that somehow, true and just
    His plans work out for mortals; not a tear
    Is shed when fortune, which the world holds
        dear,
Falls from his grasp; better, with love, a crust
Than living in dishonor; envies not,
    Nor loses faith in man; but does his best
Nor ever mourns over his humbler lot,
    But with a smile and words of hope, gives zest
To every toiler; he alone is great,
Who by a life heroic conquers fate.

SUCCESS

That man is a success who has lived well, laughed
often and loved much; who has gained the respect
of intelligent men and the love of children; who
has filled his niche and accomplished his task; who
leaves the world better than he found it, whether
by an improved poppy, a perfect poem or a rescued
soul; who never lacked appreciation of earth's beauty
or failed to express it; who looked for the best in
others and gave the best he had.

Robert Louis Stevenson

MY MOTHERS BIBLE

This book is all that's left me now,
    Tears will unbidden start,—
With faltering lip and throbbing brow
    I press it to my heart.
For many generations past,
    Here is our family tree:
My mother's hand this Bible clasped;
    She, dying, gave it me.

Ah! well do I remember those
    Whose names these records bear,
Who round the hearthstone used to close
    After the evening prayer
And speak of what these pages said,
    In tones my heart would thrill!
Though they are with the silent dead,
    Here are they living still!

My father read this holy book
    To brothers, sister, dear;
How calm was my poor mother's look,
    Who leaned God's word to hear.
Her angel face—I see it yet!
    What thronging memories come!
Again that little group is met
    Within the halls of home!

Thou truest friend man ever knew,
  Thy constancy I've tried;
Where all were false I found thee true,
  My counsellor and guide.
The mines of earth no treasure give
  That could this volume buy:
In teaching me the way to live,
  It taught me how to die.

LIFE

(A Literary Curiosity.)

Why all this toil for triumphs of an hour?

Young

Life's a short summer—man is but a flower.

Dr. Johnson

By turns we catch the fatal breath and die;

Pope

The cradle and the tomb, alas! so nigh.

Prior

To be is better far than not to be,

Sewell

Though all man's life may seem a tragedy;

Spenser

But light cares speak when mighty griefs are dumb

Daniel

The bottom is but shallow whence they come.

Sir Walter Raleigh

Thy fate is the common fate of all;

Longfellow

Unmingled joys can here no man befall;

Southwell

Nature to each allots his proper sphere,

Congreve

Fortune makes folly her peculiar care.

Churchill

Custom does often reason overrule,

Rochester

And throw a cruel sunshine on a fool.

Armstrong

56

Live well; how long or short permit to Heaven.

Milton

They who forgive most shall be most forgiven.

Bailey

Sin may be clasped so close we cannot see its face

French

Vile intercourse where virtue has no place.

Somerville

Then keep each passion down, however dear,

Thompson

Thou pendulum betwixt a smile and tear.

Byron

Her sensual snares let faithless pleasure lay,

Smollett

With craft and skill to ruin and betray.

Crabbe

Soar not too high to fall, but stoop to rise;

Massinger

We masters grow of all that we despise.

Crowley

Oh, then, renounce that impious self-esteem,

Beattie

Riches have wings and grandeur is a dream.

Cowper

Think not ambition wise because 'tis brave.

Sir Wm. Davenant

The paths of glory lead but to the grave.

Gray

What is ambition? 'Tis a glorious cheat,

Willis

Only destructive to the brave and great.

Addison

What's all the gaudy glitter of a crown?

Dryden

The way to bliss lies not on beds of down.

Francis Quarles

How long we live, not years, but actions tell;

Watkins

That man lives twice who lives the first life well.

Herrick

Make, then, while yet ye may, your God your friend,

William Mason

Whom Christians worship, yet not comprehend.

Hill

The trust that's given, guard, and to yourself be just;

Dano

For live we how we may, yet die we must.

Shakespeare

58